WILLIAM C. DIXON, JR., ED.D. &
LA' TOYA THOMAS-DIXON, ED.D.

MENTORING CAN MAKE A DIFFERENCE

ESTABLISHING RELATIONSHIPS WITH AFRICAN AMERICAN MALES

outskirts
press

Outskirts Press, Inc.
http://www.outskirtspress.com

ISBN: 978-1-4787-8431-9

PRINTED IN THE UNITED STATES OF AMERICA

Dedication

This book is dedicated to my beautiful wife, Dr. La'Toya Thomas-Dixon, who has been my biggest cheerleader through not only my dissertation journey but for inspiring me to write this book.

- Dr. William C. Dixon, Jr.

This book is dedicated to my late husband, Dr. William Dixon, Jr. Your work in education has not gone unnoticed or been forgotten. Cowriting this book with you was your dream, and now it has come true. You were a friend in education, and now your passion for the culture of African American male students will live on.

- Dr. La'Toya Thomas-Dixon

TABLE OF CONTENTS

Acknowledgements

I would like to thank my mother, Valencia Howard, for motivating and pushing me to give my best. I would also like to thank my stepfather, Jessie Howard, Jr., for assisting me with my academics during middle and high school. In addition, I would like to thank my late father, William Dixon, Sr., for always being proud of me and giving me the confidence to do well. Dr. Lynn Long of Cambridge College, who encouraged me to continue my passion for this subject. Dr. Long, you and my wife, La' Toya, gave me the spark I needed to reach this monumental point in my professional career. I cannot forget my sons, Mitchell and Xavier, my motivating factors to work harder so they could enjoy a quality life. I trust that you will use my example to give your best in everything in life.

- Dr. William C. Dixon Jr.

I would like to thank my family and closest friends, who supported my desire to complete William's book for publication. To Leila Williams, Dr. Vashti Washington, and Dr. Zona Jefferson, Superintendents of Allendale, Jasper, and Florence (4), thank you for the acknowledgment of how well William and I worked together, not only as spouses but also as colleagues in education. I will never forget your support. Thank you to Earl Choice and Dr. Ken Jenkins for taking the time to mentor William throughout his assistant superintendent role in Colleton and Cleveland County School Districts. I also appreciate your mentorship Dr. Jenkins. Dr. MiShawna Moore, you have been my inspiration in all that I have done since our work together in Charleston and Halifax Counties. I owe a lot to you; as you know, you are my rock in education. Jay Davis, thank you for continuing to mentor the CAGERS© well after 2015.

- Dr. La' Toya Thomas-Dixon-

ABOUT THE AUTHORS

Dr. William Curtis Dixon, Jr., was an educator for twenty years, primarily in the states of South and North Carolina. He started his career as a teacher and served as assistant principal, principal, and assistant superintendent, and as an adjunct professor at one university and one community college until his untimely death in April 2015. He was a father of two young men, a brother, and a husband. He served in the military for a short period and enjoyed a long career as a basketball coach. He was recognized as a State Basketball Coach of the Year twice in South Carolina. He founded the Carolina CAGERS, formerly Charleston CAGERS, an Amateur American Union basketball team for youth in third through eleventh grade in the LowCountry of South Carolina. He held a bachelor of arts degree in history education from South Carolina State University (South Carolina), a master of education degree in sports management from the United States Sports Academy (Alabama), an educational specialist degree with a specialization in educational leadership from Cambridge College (Massachusetts), and a doctoral degree with a specialization in teacher leadership from Walden University (Minnesota).

Dr. La'Toya Thomas-Dixon is an educator of eighteen years and serves as a director of curriculum and instruction, K-12, in South Carolina. She has served in the following roles: teacher, assistant principal, principal, elementary principal coach, and director of early childhood, elementary, and special projects. Dr. Thomas-Dixon is an adjunct professor at a major university and a past associate professor at several rural, state, and community colleges. She holds a bachelor of arts degree in elementary education from Columbia College (South Carolina), a master of arts in education with a specialization in Creative Arts in Learning from Lesley University (Massachusetts), an educational specialist degree in educational administration from Cambridge College (Massachusetts), and a doctorate of education in teacher leadership from Walden University (Minnesota).

INTRODUCTION

As a school district administrator, I have the challenging task of making sure all children are learning regardless of their gender, poverty level, family background, disability, race, or ethnicity. I continue to be concerned about the frightening numbers that haunt African American male students, academically and behaviorally. As a group, they achieve the lowest grades and standardized test scores. They consistently have the greatest amount of office referrals, suspensions, and absences. What's the problem? Why are African American male students struggling nationally? Why are only 53 percent of them graduating on time and receiving their high school diplomas? How can we address this issue, which has every leader and educator in our country searching for effective strategies that will counter the disturbing statistics plaguing them? African American male students are being marked as endangered, at risk, misunderstood, troubled, neglected, and even hopeless. Pedro Noguera in 1997 noted that just hearing the words *black* and *male* automatically puts a Black male at the end of the spectrum, which causes vulnerability and makes them least desired by society.

One of the most disappointing times in my young life was during the separation and divorce of my parents. Only twelve years old, I was devastated. My mom received custody of my brother and me. I was afraid that I would not see my dad anymore. In grade school, my grades began to suffer. At home I was quiet and withdrawn, to the point of hiding under my bed in the room I shared with my brother. I will never forget the evening that my dad came to our house after the divorce and made me come from under the bed. He pretty much assured me that he would remain a part of my brother's and my life. My brother and I were able to spend two weekends per month with our dad. As time passed, my mom eventually remarried, and my stepfather took an active role in our lives. Along with my mom, he made sure we attended church together.

He checked our homework, tossed the football and shot the basketball with us, and gave us allowance when we completed our chores. Although he did not try to replace my dad, it was good for two African American boys to have two strong men in our lives. My brother and I could have easily become the statistics that victimize fatherless children, statistics that President Barack Obama included in his 2008 Father's Day speech that noted children without a father are (1) five times more likely to commit a crime or live in poverty, (2) nine times more likely to drop out of school, and (3) twenty times more likely to end up in prison.

During my senior year in high school, I became acquainted with an African American physical education and health teacher who was hired as an assistant track and field coach. The assistant track and field coach took a strong interest in my best friend and me. During my high school academic career, my only African American teacher was a female US history instructor, who simply did not have a relationship beyond the classroom with most of her students, specifically African American boys. In our local school system, African American male teachers were rare. The assistant track and field coach was only the second African American male teacher employed at my high school. The high school also had a veteran vocational education teacher who was an African American male. The other African American male teacher in our school system was a sixth grade science teacher. When our high school hired the new the assistant track and field coach, most African American students were proud to have someone who looked like them. Nationwide the numbers are still dismal, with only 7 percent of all public school teachers being African American Only 1 percent of all public school teachers are African American males.

My best friend and I had been starters on our school's basketball team and had ambitions to play college basketball. Although the assistant track and field coach was not our high school basketball coach, he picked us up one evening, along with another college basketball prospect from a neighboring school. We spent the night with him and his family in their home and the next morning traveled to visit a small college in South Carolina. This institution was designated as a Historical Black College and University (HBCU). My high school guidance counselor, a Caucasian woman, advised me not to attend an HBCU, noting that it would be hard to get a good job when I graduated. Her comments always stayed with me, particularly since three uncles, an aunt, and two first cousins had attended HBCUs before I graduated from high school (and one uncle eventually attended law school and worked on Capitol Hill in Washington).

My best friend and I had a great visit and workout with the basketball staff. I will never forget the head college basketball coach calling us into his office and saying that he wanted us to play basketball on this team. While neither one of us ever signed or attended the college (my parents' income was too much for a full grant in aid, and I had to pay more than I would at a state-supported school), our assistant track and field coach's generous act, taking us to a college basketball workout, was never forgotten. I decided to attend a larger college in the same city that was less expensive. I was somewhat familiar with the school since two uncles, an aunt, and a first cousin had attended it previously. In addition, my stepfather and mother had taken my brother and me to the school's homecoming football weekend to visit with their friends of several years. My best friend eventually committed to another small HBCU and joined the United States Army, and the college basketball prospect who joined us for the visit and workout was killed in a car accident before high school graduation. Through this experience of being assisted by the assistant track and field coach, I developed a commitment to help other young people, especially African American boys who aspired to attend college or play sports in college. Even before I graduated from college, I was taking my brother to college visits and workouts at HBCUs. Furthermore, I made a commitment to take boys to college basketball tryouts, as well as write and send athletic letters and resumes for boys and girls in many sports throughout my professional career. It all began because of my experience with my assistant track and field coach from high school, an African American man who made a difference in my life.

During my second year as a classroom teacher, I saw a need for additional support for African American male students. Early one morning before the start of school, a young African American male student entered the school in which I worked, walked into the cafeteria, and viscously attacked another African American male student with a knife. The victim suffered serious injuries and was airlifted to a hospital in a major city one hour away. The incident was carried over from a conflict the two students had had during the weekend. I questioned what could make a student so upset that he would commit such a violent act? I wondered if the student had someone he could have talked to or someone who could have helped him offset some of the anger that consumed him from the weekend incident.

Earlier in the semester, my fraternity brother, who was also my work colleague and roommate, joined me in starting a group called Technique. Through this group, we could meet with fifteen identified young men, all African American juniors and seniors, and provide them with coping skills to be more successful socially and academically. We met weekly and quickly established the group as one of the more popular "clubs" on campus. Technique members cooked breakfast for the teachers during in-service days, played bingo with elders at a local nursing home, tutored elementary students, and participated in school assembly programs and pep rallies.

As members of Omega Psi Phi Fraternity, we knew we were impacting the Technique members in a positive way. The school and the town in which we lived were in rural settings. There was not much to do, and we were located far from our family and closest friends. The Technique club members became our "little brothers" and "extended family." They visited our classrooms after school. We played basketball together and, with school support and parent consent, hosted a Super Bowl gathering at our home. The Technique club was so successful that we began a freshmen and sophomore group called LifeQuest. My fraternity brother and I were considered "rising stars" at the school because we could take African American male students who were once classroom disruptions and academic casualties and transform them into school leaders with college aspirations.

Unfortunately, my fraternity brother and I left the school after one year. As young teachers, there simply was not much to do in a small rural community, and we were afforded opportunities to grow professionally in larger settings. I accepted a job as head varsity boys' basketball coach, which had been a dream of mine since high school. Although we reluctantly walked away from Technique and LifeQuest, the young men from both clubs kept in touch with us, and we reconnected through Facebook. Twenty-nine of the thirty young men graduated from high school, with many of them going on to college and the military. (Unfortunately one LifeQuest member died from a fatal car accident before graduating.) Several of the members pledged into fraternities and became educators themselves. Although I have worked in various schools and school districts in my career, I have maintained my commitment to make a difference with African American male students. I began a group called the Young Gents as a junior high school teacher, with focuses similar to those in Technique and LifeQuest. Despite growing responsibilities as an assistant principal and principal, I continued Young Gents at schools in which I worked. I saw the need. The need for African American male students to have a role model. The need for African American male students to have the guidance and encouragement necessary to be successful. The need for African American male students to have the exposure and experiences to want to do better, to want to go places.

During my transition from the classroom to administration, I began a study on African American male students. The purpose of the nineteen-week study was to determine if mentoring was effective in improving the academic achievement of African American male students. To evaluate the effect of mentoring, participants engaged in a weekly after-school program that provided initiatives to improve academics and social responsiveness. I did a similar study eight years later in my role as a district administrator. The purpose of that eight-week study was to determine if mentoring would affect the academic performance of African American male students. Like the first study, mentors focused on providing initiatives to improve grades in an attempt to influence young men to become better students. In both studies, I saw how mentoring made a difference with African American male students. Examples of established mentoring programs are Big Brothers/Big Sisters, Help One Student to Succeed, 100 Black Men of America, Inc., Let Each One Teach One, and the National Mentoring Partnership.

While this book will provide a general overview of those programs, I will share how anyone who wants to make a difference with African American male students can be a mentor or establish his or her own mentoring program. My findings prompted me to write this book and share with all stakeholders the four factors that are associated with the academic performance of African American male students and the benefits that mentoring can have in overcoming them. During a time when we are losing more and more African American male students, it is essential that all Americans be concerned. It is time for each of us to do something to make a difference and avoid African American males becoming an endangered species. Mentoring can be a giant step in helping African American male students to maximize their full potential.

Chapter 1
THERE IS A NATIONWIDE PROBLEM

AFRICAN AMERICAN MALE students are consistently performing below average in schools. Currently, they are last in academic performance, and first in discipline problems, out of school suspensions, and poor attendance. Urban sociologist and professor Pedro Noguera reported in *The Trouble with Black Boys: And Other Reflections on Race, Equity, and the Future of Public Education,* that the labels of at-risk, endangered, and series of crisis have been often labeled to African American males. Noguera said that just to hear the words *black* and *male* automatically puts an African American male at the end of the spectrum, which causes vulnerability and the feeling that they are least desired by society.

Per the Black Boys Report, the national graduation rate for African American male students in 2009–2010 was 52 percent while the graduation rate for Caucasian male students was 78 percent. The National Assessment of Education Progress (NAEP) reported that in 2005 and 2007, African American male students in fourth grade scored lower than every other gender and ethnic group. African American male students averaged 195 in 2005 and 199 in 2007, and African American female students averaged 205 and 208. Caucasian American male students averaged 226 and 228; Caucasian American female students averaged 232 and 234. Hispanic American male students averaged 200 and 202; Hispanic American female students averaged 205 and 208. And Asian American male students averaged 225 and 228; and Asian American female students averaged 232 and 236.

Dr. Ivory Toldson noted in the *Journal of Negro Education* (2012) that 45 percent of African American men have attempted college, but only 16 percent have a four-year degree. In comparison, 32 percent of Caucasian men and 20 percent of African American females have completed college with a four-year degree. The National Center of Education Statistics (2010) listed the dropout rate of African American male students as 9 percent, which is twice the dropout rate of Caucasian male students.

Evidence indicates that African American children, especially males, are far more likely than any other group to break school rules, disrupting their own and their classmates' education. African American male students consistently have the greatest amount of office referrals, suspensions, and absences. African American male students are two and half times as likely to be disciplined as Caucasian and Hispanic Americans and five times as likely as Asian Americans, although they make up only 12 percent of the population. In many classrooms, African American male students are unjustly singled out for punishment. Abigail Thernstrom and Stephan Thernstrom suggested in their book *No Excuses: Closing the Racial Gap in Learning* that Caucasian Americans in authority are unfamiliar and even uncomfortable with the more active and physical style of communication that characterizes African American adolescents. The impassioned and emotive manner popular among young African Americans may be interpreted as combative or argumentative by unfamiliar listeners.

As a district administrator, I once attended a leadership retreat in which the school's data revealed that African American students received 4,881 referrals compared to 1,522 referrals for Caucasian students. The 4,881 referrals accounted for 5,580 days lost in instruction, including 3,717 days out-of-school suspension. In comparison, the Caucasian students lost 1,536 days of instruction and 914 days out-of-school suspension. In this school, African Americans received four times as many suspension days as their Caucasian peers, even though the student population was 52 percent African American and 44 percent Caucasian. Research has found that learning is impacted by behavior. It was not surprising to discover that African American male students were the lowest performing subgroup in this school. Similar trends were identified at the alternative school. Students were placed at the alternative school for poor behavior. Recently, the school's total population was 112 students. According to school reports, 97 of them were African American male students! How do such disturbing trends continue to haunt public schools across America?

In my research, I determined that African American male students' poor performance in academics has been attributed to peer pressure, socioeconomic status, societal issues, and the lack of a long-term caring adult. In addition, there is a growing shortage of minority teachers. In many public schools across the United States, there is not one African American teacher. Approximately 40 percent of the students in America will never have an African American teacher during their prekindergarten through twelfth grade experience. This shortage has educators concerned about the impact of fewer role models for minority students and the potential loss of cultural understanding of all students. As prekindergarten through twelfth grade schools become more diverse in America, exposing students to various types of role models will be important.

African American male students have been found to benefit from male role models. Recent studies suggest that African American male students need to see African Americans in positions of leadership because such role models provide them with aspirations to become successful. But with a shortage of minority male teachers, school districts nationwide have established rigorous initiatives to reach African American male students, such as implementing year-round schooling, changing the hours of the school day, reducing class size, emphasizing technology, creating one-on-one programs, and organizing single gender classrooms. I believe mentoring can be another important initiative. My studies noted that a growing number of evaluations suggest that planned mentoring relationships can positively influence a range of outcomes, including improvements in peer and parental relationships, academic achievement, and self-concept. Leon Dappen and Jody Iserhagen elaborated in a 2006 *Urban Education* article titled "Urban and Nonurban Schools: Examination of a Statewide Student Mentoring Program" that school mentoring programs are assisting in the reduction of alcohol and drug use, teenage parentage, gang membership, and peer violence.

African American male students continue to be challenges in classrooms across the United States. Educators have instituted various programs to address the struggles of the African American male student academically. Despite these initiatives, schools must continue to find ways to motivate and develop the full academic potential of African American male students. Various factors have been associated with the academic performance of African American male students. In the next chapter, I will discuss what I believe is the first identified factor: **peer pressure**.

Chapter 2
PEER PRESSURE

AFRICAN AMERICAN MALES are greatly influenced by their peers. Middle-class African Americans who try to encourage their children to excel in school often experience challenges to engage in nonacademic interests due to peer pressure. Plain and simple, in many facets of African American culture, academic success and popularity are not always appropriate when placed together. Specifically, among African American male students, receiving good grades is considered "punking out" or acting white. Gifted and talented African American male students often sell themselves short and are pressured to minimize their capability and potential in order to be acknowledged by their "homies," "broheims," or "dawgs."

As an advanced placement student at my high school in the 1980s, I struggled with peer pressure. Often I acted as a class clown to overcome the "acting white" label. In many classes, I gave minimal effort and participated in more popular behaviors to fit in with my peers. During advanced placement classes in my grade level, I was the only African American male student. When I took classes with the next grade level of students, I sat at the back of the room, passed notes, and told jokes to make everyone laugh. I did not hang with my classmates at lunch or on break. I found other African American male students, mostly athletes, to hang with, play basketball with, or mingle with the prettiest girls. I did not want to be associated with a nerdy or "copping out" reputation. I valued my peer group's opinion of me.

Fortunately, I had strong parents who did not allow me much leverage away from school. When my peers went to clubs on weekends, my "crew" and I would show up at 10:00 p.m. As an eleventh grader, my curfew was 11:00 p.m., which was the time that most people arrived at the club. We arrived so early that the disc jockey (DJ) had not even set up yet. As my peers drove up, I would be pulling off at 10:45 p.m., stating that we were going to the store before it closed to get some food or beer. Of course, my peers had no idea that we would not be returning. Pulling out of the club driveway, I sped off to drop off my crew and rush home to my parents before the eleven o'clock deadline. Arriving home even shortly after eleven often led to long lectures or nagging from my parents or being grounded, which meant no phone rights (cell phones didn't exist yet), no going out, and no driving unless it was to school. When we returned to school on Monday mornings, each of the club attendees would boast and brag about the liveliness at the club. They would ask what happened to me, and I would reply, "Man, I got up with this chick ... you know how I do." Lying kept me credible with the boys, specifically with the African American males who were regarded as cool, hip, and hard.

During my first year as a teacher, I attended the school's first quarterly awards program. All of the students in the school were invited to watch their peers receive recognition for good grades, behavior, and attendance. The principal believed it would be ideal for the entire student body to witness the awards program. He felt students without awards would be motivated to do better by watching their peers receive various incentives, such as cups of candy, certificates for restaurant meals, T-shirts, and Walkmans. The opposite occurred. Students who received awards were embarrassingly booed. At one point in the program, the two African American male students whose names were called for receiving all As refused to stand or go to the podium. The principal refused to give them their awards after the program because they did not come up when their names were initially called. One of the African American male students tried to convince the principal that he was in the restroom when his name was called. However, he was observed slumped over in the bleachers to avoid the chorus of jeers. Future quarterly awards programs included the awardees and their parents only. Teachers were required to stay in their rooms and supervise the remaining students. I remember a frustrated colleague scolding an African American female awardee when she returned from an awards program for giving her candy to an African American male classmate. Her words were "If he didn't earn it, don't give it to him!"

In the classroom, many African American male students tend to act out to get attention from their peers. Showing off and disrupting the class establishes creditability. The desire to be accepted as one of the boys is more valued than meeting Common Core, College and Career Ready, or state standards. As a district administrator, I was responsible for observing classrooms and providing feedback to help teachers to be successful. I visited a seventh grade class one morning where a Caucasian female teacher was teaching English Language Arts. One African American male student was disturbing the class. Each time the teacher asked a question, he blurted out without being called on. Finally, she lost her composure and raised her voice for the young man to be quiet. Many of the remaining students, African American and Caucasian, were also bothered.

I whispered to two students, "Does he always do this?"

And their answer was yes. I exited the classroom, but before doing so, I called for the young man to join me outside in the hallway. He looked surprised but was compliant. Outside I introduced myself and asked him his name. He willingly responded.

I asked him, "Why are you wasting your time and your life?" He somewhat dropped his head.

I nicely asked him to look at me. Noticing how big he was, I said, "Do you play sports?"

He replied, "Yes sir, football."

I inquired, "So you want to be a pro football player, huh?"

He nodded his head in agreement and said, "Yes sir."

I shared, "Well, you do know that you will need this class and your education if you plan on getting a scholarship to play football in college."

He looked at me attentively as though no one else had ever had this discussion with him.

I continued, "You have a wonderful opportunity, but you are trying to be a class clown. You are a big guy so people already see you. Let them see you now for how smart you are and stop wasting your ability."

He responded, "Yes sir."

Knowing his coaches, I said, "Do I need to talk to your coaches? What would they say at practice today if they knew you were joking around and disturbing everyone else from getting their work done, giving this teacher a hard time?"

He said, "They wouldn't like it."

I elaborated, "She worked for hours this weekend to get this lesson prepared for you and your classmates, and you're messing around. I trust that I will not hear anything else about you disturbing the class and disrespecting her."

He replied, "Yes sir."

I shook his hand, patted him on the back, and he returned to the classroom.

Surprisingly, I noted a similar situation in a high school math class. The teacher was giving an overview of his expectations and requirements for the course. One of the requirements was for students to purchase a calculator. The average price of the required calculator was between eighty and ninety dollars.

As a measure to support students with financial difficulty, the school's math department offered used calculators for a five-dollar rental fee for the entire year. The teacher, an African American man, noted that this was a "super deal."

A senior African American male student yelled out, "Five dollars! Man, I ain't wasting no five dollars on no calculator."

Several of his classmates, mostly African American, laughed at his statement. The teacher caught himself and did not respond.

Another African American male student expressed, "Man, you stupid."

The senior African American male student said, "Bo, I don't care. I ain't paying no five dollars for no calculator."

I exited the classroom, and as I did with the middle school student, I asked the senior African American male student to join me in the hallway. As he left his desk, the teacher asked, "Where are you going?"

I answered, "I got him."

Outside I said, "Do you know who I am?"

He responded, "The principal?"

I replied, "No sir." I introduced myself and shared my job title and my responsibilities in the school district.

He said, "Okay,"

I asked, "Do you know why I called you out here?"

He answered, "No sir."

I remarked, "Was that really necessary?"

He looked puzzled.

I noted, "To yell out like that."

He said, "I am sorry, but that is a lot of money."

"What grade are you in and what do you want to do with your life?" I asked.

He stated, "I'm a senior and I don't know."

I chuckled. "You a senior acting like that? I expect a freshman to act like that but a senior, especially over five dollars."

He looked at me in disbelief as I chuckled.

"Let's see five dollars versus ninety dollars … sounds pretty easy to me," I said. "Plus, just fifty years ago (referencing segregated schools in the South), students who looked just like you and me did not have calculators or even the chance to get an equal education. Now you guys have everything and don't appreciate it. You owe those who struggled and paved the way for you and me to be better than that."

He said, "I guess you right."

I looked around and replied, "Sadly, you did all of this in front of a black male teacher. Disrespecting any teacher is wrong but …"

"What do you mean?" he asked.

I answered, "Simple. What are you?"

He hesitantly stated, "Black."

I elaborated, "You are fortunate. I never had a black male teacher in high school, and if I did, I wouldn't put him on the spot like that. You lucky that he didn't write you up."

He said, "I got you."

The bell rang for the class to be dismissed. As students exited the classroom, they saw him talking to me. As expected, several of his African American male friends laughed.

I asked, "Is there something you need to do?"

He left me, returned to the classroom, found the teacher, and said, "I am sorry." He began to go into some detail about why he was sorry. I left and allowed the teacher and him to continue their conversation.

The experiences that I shared with the two young men are just snapshots of what occurs every day in thousands of classrooms across the country. However, in most cases, the hallway conversation does not take place. The "relationship" aspect is often missing. African American males can be successful especially when they are respected and reprimanded without bringing more attention to the situation. Many teachers with increasing pressures to improve test scores simply do not have the time to address each African American male student who may be off task. Writing referrals and sending them to the office are more convenient options.

In the next chapter, I will discuss the second identified factor that impacts the academic performance of African American male students: **socioeconomic status**.

Chapter 3

SOCIOECONOMIC STATUS

OFTEN, BUT NOT always, low-performing African American male students come from a poor socioeconomic background. The problems that impact African American male students are more commonplace and widespread in areas subject to poverty. Such areas are frequently underdeveloped with limited resources and lack a supporting economy. Crime is typically excessive in poverty-infested neighborhoods and exposure to drugs, prostitution, and murder is likely. During one of my principalships, I led a school that was in such a neighborhood. Over 99 percent of our students qualified for free and reduced lunches. Many African American male students who reside in such areas are forced to grow up before their peers and learn the necessary survival skills to make it in life. Doing well in school becomes an afterthought and of lesser importance.

One morning, as I was preparing for work, I turned on the television news as I typically did. The news coverage focused on a dead body that was found downtown. I was putting on my shoes around 6:30 a.m. and was very interested in this story. A dead body had been discovered on a busy street near the school where I was the principal. I quickly thought about my students because many of them walked to school alone or with a few peers. I rushed to school to make sure our students did not see the body. When I arrived, policemen were on the scene. Unfortunately, several early birds had already seen and stepped over the body. Our students were accustomed to seeing drunks passed out along the streets, nightwalkers jumping in and out of cars in the early morning hours, and drug dealers standing on the corner to make the next sale. However, I did not want them to see a dead body before going to class. Our guidance counselor and parent educator provided counseling to the students who needed it on this day, but I was bothered by what they saw. Nonetheless, our children were resilient, and in high-poverty environments such occurrences are often the norm.

School did not officially open until 7:15 a.m. for breakfast, but my staff and I learned quickly to allow our students to enter earlier to ensure their safety and make sure they were warm. Several parents who drove their children to school dropped them off early as well. Getting to work and making ends meet was a priority. Often our teachers were inconvenienced by beginning morning duties earlier than most of their colleagues in other schools, but they knew our school served as a safe haven for our students.

Many African American children from poverty-stricken environments spend countless and meaningless hours in front of the television. Entertainment, not school, appears to be a priority. In *No Excuses: Closing the Racial Gap in Learning,* Abigail Thernstrom and Stephan Thernstrom reported that nearly half of African American fourth graders spent five hours or more watching television on a typical school day. Despite the greater demands of academics in twelfth grade, one third of African Americans were still watching television for five hours or more daily. Frequently, watching television can be attributed to living in single-parent families, in which the parent works various jobs to support the family. Regularly, in poverty-infested neighborhoods, African American males identify with rap artists because they look like them and admire their fame and wealth. They see the rap industry as a fast way out of poverty. African American boys who struggle in school are fond of rap artists because many of them also did poorly in school but still became successful because of their music. I will discuss African American males and rap artists in more detail in chapter four.

African American children often arrive at school less academically prepared than their Caucasian American counterparts. Many African American male students cannot prosper in current school programs because they lack support at home, often coming from single-parent families. Often in such homes, many African American males have single mothers who must work two or three part-time jobs to make ends meet. Many single-parent families have no option but to reside in low-income housing in impoverished neighborhoods. Seeking a feeling of self-identity, some African American males in these neighborhoods are motivated to associate with drug dealers and gang leaders and consider them role models. The domination, control, and money possessed is greatly respected and idolized by African American males in search of themselves. They may conclude as early as their elementary years that they do not need school because they can pocket money quickly through unlawful business. This unlawful business, which may include dealing drugs, breaking into homes, or robbing people, can quickly lead to an early life of crime and jail time.

During my first principalship, I had young men as early as second grade serve as drug runners for their older brothers, uncles, cousins, and often their fathers. I remember countless incidents involving desperate single mothers trying to save their elementary-age sons. These mothers were doing the best they could and often turned to me and my staff for assistance. I, along with my guidance counselor and student concern specialist, spent long hours meeting with our boys and trying to save them from the streets of poverty. A few years after I left the school, I was horrified to discover that one of my former African American male students whom we tried to save was tragically shot and murdered, thrown out of a car, and left for dead along a busy highway underpass. Most recently, another former African American male student, from the same school and poverty environment, was shot and killed by a policeman in an incident that gained statewide coverage. This occurred just months before the controversial Ferguson, Missouri, case in August 2014, involving an African American male teenager, Michael Brown, and a white policeman, Darren Wilson, which received nationwide coverage.

In a "Call for Change: The Social and Educational Factors Contributing to the Outcomes of Black Males in Urban Schools," authors Sharon Lewis, Candace Simon, Renata Uzzell, Amanda Horwitz, and Michael Casserly reported that African American males ages eighteen and over accounted for 5 percent of the total college student population and 36 percent of the total prison population. In 2002, Ellis Cose stated in *The Envy of the World: On Being a Black Man in America* that 792,000 African American males were in United States prisons in June 2000 and one in four African American boys will spend at least part of their life locked down. Judith Kleinfeld highlighted in her book "The State of American Boyhood" (2009) similar disturbing trends, including 17 percent of African American males ages sixteen to twenty-four are disconnected (those not in school or the workplace) compared to 4 percent of Caucasian American males the same age.

In the midst of completing this book, I met a twelve-year-old African American male student who was recommended for expulsion after bringing a BB gun that resembled a real gun to school for the third time. When I met with the student, he was accompanied by his grandfather, who had just retired as a truck driver, and a family friend who called herself the student's "auntie." The student could not explain why he brought the gun to school. I shared with the family that laws require school administrators to take such incidents seriously and that they could not afford to overlook the behavior with safety being a priority. I felt bad for the young man. He was a good-looking kid and appeared to have a great deal of potential. I wondered what was going on in his life. Where was his father? Where was his mother? It appeared he made these choices to get attention even at the expense of being expelled and going to juvenile justice.

During a middle school faculty meeting, teachers were discussing a book study in relation to African American males. The principal asked the teachers to share why they thought African American males were doing poorly. There were many comments.

One teacher replied, "They lack basic skills. They only know five-letter words. My second grade daughter has a stronger vocabulary." Many of the African American female teachers took offense to such strong comments, based on their gestures. Another teacher said, "Broken homes with single-parent families, often the mother, a grandparent, or another guardian." And a third teacher suggested, "Many times these single parents have to go to work at four thirty in the morning and don't get home until seven thirty at night. By the time they get home, they are tired and unable to give their children the attention that they need."

As I listened to the responses, I couldn't help but relate to each of the comments to socioeconomic status. Single parents must work to provide for their children. Many single parents do the best they can without support from a second parent or other family members. And although I also had strong concerns with the first teacher's comments, comparing her second grade daughter's vocabulary to that of middle school African American males in her classes, I concluded that academics can be impacted without parental support at home. These are often characteristics of African American homes in such environments where survival is more important than school.

In the next chapter, I will discuss the increasing **societal issues that plague African American male students.** While other groups are also impacted by these issues, African American males appear to allow them to disrupt their academic performance at a much more alarming rate.

Chapter 4
SOCIETAL ISSUES

SOCIETAL ISSUES HAVE also been linked to poor school performance among African American male students. African American male students in their preteen to teenage years choose images of hipness and swag that many African American males use to express themselves. Culture, the entertainment industry, social networks, and adults give young African American men negative messages about their potential and talents. These societal issues include urban music, professional sports, and relationships.

In search of role models and finding their own self-image, many African American males have turned to rap artists in the music industry. As a district administrator, one of my responsibilities was meeting with students and parents attempting to enroll them in school. In one particular meeting, I met with a young man and his father. The father had recently gained custody of the young man. The young man had been in and out of trouble, bouncing from school to school and juvenile justice. After running away and staying out of school for nearly a year, the young man left his mother to live with his father. When I asked the young man why I should let him back in school, he openly expressed that he just wanted to go to school until his seventeenth birthday; he had plans to go to Atlanta to make a name for himself in the rap industry. I shared with him the value of an education and earning a high school diploma or credential. I told him that he had a right to pursue a career as a rapper, but he needed a backup plan. I preached that he should use his education to make a way until he made it as a rapper. He responded that he was going to make it and no one was going to stop him. He stated that Young Scooter, an up-and-coming Atlanta-based rapper with a criminal record was going to look out for him and that the rapper liked this young man's freestyling.

Despite my urging, the young man insisted he knew what he was doing and that no one, including me or his father, could stop him from making it big. I shared that there was nothing wrong with him dreaming and pursuing a rap career. However, I reminded him that most potential rappers do not make it big in the industry. I emphasized that, like him, there were thousands of young people who had the same dream, the same ambition. According to a source on the TR Shady website, successful rappers make a modest $1.25 per album and only average three cents per single CD.

During a meeting with two colleagues to discuss gang prevention, I was shown a locally created rap video made by several African American males promoting violence. The video was placed on YouTube and glorified the life of a local gang in their "hood." The gang dissed rival gangs and even made a mockery of the police walking through their hood as they investigated several shootings and crimes involving gang members. Disturbingly, the rap video captured the faces of each of the members, some holding and cocking guns, and all of them were African American males who had dropped out of high school. Sadly, the streets had consumed them and they relied on a life of crime, including harming and killing others. Younger African American boys idolized them and viewed the rap video as a quick payday to stardom.

Athletics hold a similar appeal for many African American males. These young men by the thousands have expectations that their athletic talents will lead to a college scholarship in a premier division one program and eventually a professional contract in the National Basketball Association (NBA) or National Football League (NFL). Through the media and the unfair expectations of their families, who may believe their son's recreation or school team successes will lead to a big payday, African American boys are faced with the harsh reality that their professional ambitions are difficult at best. African American boys think they can become rich without academic success. They have false perceptions that playing professionally at a young age, often without a high school or college diploma, is the norm since they idolize a younger generation of stars in the NBA and NFL.

African American boys nationwide want to be the next LeBron James, Kobe Bryant, Kevin Durant, Derrick Rose, or Carmelo Anthony in the NBA. There is a very slim chance of making it to the NBA. Like many African American boys today, I dreamed of playing in the NBA. In elementary and middle school, after homework and chores, I pretended to be yesteryear's stars on my backyard dirt court. I did my best impressions of Magic Johnson, Julius Irving, Kareem Abdul-Jabbar, Moses Malone, and Dominique Wilkins. I started playing organized basketball late but was a good high school player. However, as I got older, my dreams were suddenly shot down when I saw players who were bigger, stronger, quicker, and more skilled than me. Although I was a tall (six foot four) and a good player back home, as I competed abroad, I quickly discovered that I wasn't as tall, as quick, or as skilled. Point guards were my size at some schools.

MENTORING CAN MAKE A DIFFERENCE

My dream ended as a sophomore in college, and I began to recognize that there was life after sports. Fortunately, for the most part, I was serious about my academics too and had a strong upbringing. Therefore, my transition from student athlete to student was easier to accept. Sadly, many African American male students do not take school seriously until after their professional dream has faded.

Tied to the NBA are the expensive shoes endorsed by the game's best players. African American boys from poor, middle-class, and affluent backgrounds want such shoes in elementary, middle, and high school. Owning and wearing these shoes builds creditability, status, and popularity. Many parents, including yours truly, have felt the pressure and burden of purchasing these shoes, often costing over $200, for our children to be accepted within their peer and social groups. I am often amazed at the parents and boys who will wait in long lines to buy such shoes but will not attend PTO meetings or visit their child's teachers at an open house to check on their academic progress.

According to most sources, the odds of a high school player making the NBA are between 0.03 percent and 0.04 percent. When I give presentations to youth groups, I always ask the boys how many of them want to be professional basketball players. I explain that there are fifteen players on a basketball team in high school. In South Carolina, there are approximately two hundred public high school teams, which add up to three thousand players. I always remind youth groups that there are forty-nine other states and most have larger populations than South Carolina. So, nationwide, there are about half a million players in high school boys' basketball. Next I tell them that there are over three hundred division one National Collegiate Athletic Association (NCAA) colleges in the United States. On the average roster there are twelve scholarship players, which add up to six thousand players. Things get pretty interesting when I share with them that there are also hundreds of NCAA division two and three, National Association of Intercollegiate Athletics (NAIA) and junior college teams with similar rosters. According to NCAA research in 2012, only 3.3 percent of senior boys' basketball players go on to play major college basketball.

Then the aha moment. I let them know that there are thirty NBA teams and that they have just two rounds in which only sixty players total are taken in the draft. Typically, these drafts include multiple foreign and NBA development players. The knockout punch: on average, only forty of the sixty players drafted ever make an NBA roster. Why? Because they are also competing with free agents and unsigned veterans who want to continue their NBA careers. Although the NBA's 450 players consist of mostly African Americans, eighty-four foreign players were on rosters to begin the 2012–2013 season. According to the NBA, eight of the fifteen players on the San

Antonio Spurs, the league's runner-up that season and champions in 2013–2014, were born outside of the United States.

In the NFL, African American boys envision being the next Robert "RG3" Griffin, Cam Newton, Dez Bryant, Reggie Bush, Calvin Johnson, or A. J. Green. In 2012, NCAA research reported that there were about 1.1 million boys playing high school football but only 6.4 percent were fortunate enough to play major college football. In addition, only 1.6 percent of NCAA college football players made it to the NFL. According to the NFL's corporate communications department, approximately 46 percent of current NFL players have a college degree. Only 20 percent of the league's players have a career that lasts beyond four years. Yet the players with a college degree have careers that last 50 percent longer. Although underclassmen college football players are entering the NFL draft in higher numbers, such players, who are eventually cut, will make $600,000 less than a college graduate who gets cut from the NFL. Ultimately, most African American boys simply do not understand how hard it is to make it professionally. Without the guidance of role models to help them understand the likelihood of making it professionally, many continue to write off a good education for lofty professional sports aspirations.

Most African American boys have a strong interest in girls by the time they reach middle school. This interest can impact African American boys' focus on academics. As a coach and mentor for middle-school African American youth, I have witnessed firsthand how pretty, shapely females can command the attention of African American boys. Sexuality as early as middle school age is very real in the African American culture, particularly in single-parent and broken homes. African American males are turned on by the female body and often cannot control staring, lusting, or making derogatory remarks when a nice-looking young lady passes by. It has not helped that young ladies are showing more and leaving little for the imagination.

I became familiar with a situation in which a high-school-age African American male student had sexual relations with a middle-school-age African American female student. The two students planned the event in a vacant classroom during the school day, while their African American peers served as the lookouts. Once the issue was brought to the attention of the school administration, both students were suspended and recommended for expulsion. Law enforcement was involved, and the male student went to jail because he was of age. The young man was expelled from school, served a long jail term, and registered as a sexual offender. Great potential thrown away.

A similar situation occurred years earlier when I was a teacher and coach. One afternoon, before a game, three student athletes, all African American males, left a supervised area to have sexual relations with an African American female student.

Based on reports, one of the student athletes participated in a sexual act with her, and the remaining two had plans to do so as well. However, this did not occur because the young men had to leave earlier than planned for team meetings. Several weeks later the incident was reported to the school administration and me. I was devastated. After all, I had faithfully emphasized self-discipline and self-respect with my young men. Although the student athletes lived in single-parent households, they had strong mothers who were very involved and supportive of their education.

Each of the student athletes was arrested. The two seventeen-year-olds went to jail, and the sixteen-year-old was released to his family. The young lady eventually transferred. Both seventeen-year-olds were highly regarded players. However, basketball was an afterthought with sexual assault charges. Both seventeen-year-olds completed pretrial intervention programs, which gave them opportunities to have their records expunged. Only one student athlete was able to return to the team to finish the season. Ultimately, the three student athletes attended college to play basketball. I attributed this to our program's emphasis on college exposure as early as the freshman year for our players, as well as for their family support systems. Both seventeen-year-olds eventually graduated and earned their bachelor degrees. However, the ordeal caused major duress and unnecessary disruption for the team, the school, and their lives. Equally important, the young lady suffered a traumatic experience that ultimately led to her leaving the state. The incident served as a strong reminder that even African American males with solid support can make poor choices due to the desire to be with a pretty girl and to earn sexual creditability with their peers.

In chapter 5, I will discuss the fourth factor that impacts the academic achievement of African American male students: **the lack of a long-term caring adult**. African American males can experience success if they overcome peer pressure and societal issue while growing up in a poor environment, and if they have the right support, no matter if the home has one or two parents. However, without a long-term caring adult, the odds will be more difficult.

Chapter 5
LACK OF A LONG-TERM CARING ADULT

THE FOURTH FACTOR associated with African American boys' poor academic performance has been the lack of a long-term, caring adult. Schools, extended families, and neighborhoods have changed in ways that have dramatically reduced the availability of caring adults. Noticeable in many African American homes is the absence of the father. A demographic research study (2003) noted that 32 percent of African American couples divorce as compared with 21 percent of Caucasian and 22 percent of Hispanic couples. Researchers Dr. R. Kelly Raley and Dr. Larry Bumpass reported that 70 percent of African American women's first marriages will end in divorce compared to 47 percent for Caucasian women. Several reasons lead to a higher divorce right for African Americans, which likely include age, education, and income.

Researchers Lorraine Blackman, Obie Clayton, Norval Glenn, Linda Malone-Colon, and Alex Roberts conducted a study titled "The Consequences of Marriage for African Americans" in 2005 and found that marriage results in important benefits for African American children. Divorce 360's Dr. Pamela Thompson noted that there is a 70 percent chance that a person will be born to an unmarried couple in the African American community. Many African American males are born out of wedlock, often with few positive male figures in their lives. In 2002, Dorothy Garrison-Wade and Chance Lewis concluded in "Tips for Principals and Teachers: Helping Black Students Achieve," from the book *White Teachers/Diverse Classrooms*, that only 32 percent of African American youth had fathers at home.

Complicating the absence of the father in the African American family are jail and prison sentences. According to the Sentencing Project in 2009, prison statistics illustrated that more than four in ten fathers were African American, about three in ten were Caucasian, and about two in ten were Hispanic. The Sentencing Project also

18

reported that an estimated 1.6 million children had a father in prison in mid-2007 and nearly half (46 percent) were children of African American fathers.

African American men are also missing in our nation's classrooms and schools. Garrison-Wade and Lewis pointed out that African American students are being educated by people who are not of their race or cultural background. Such circumstances do not afford African American students many opportunities to have teachers who understand their culture, communities, or learning needs. Former United States Secretary of Education Arne Duncan spearheaded the TEACH campaign to raise awareness of the teaching profession and to get a new generation of African Americans into the classroom. Duncan indicated that there are not enough African American teachers and shared that there is a "growing imbalance in terms of what our teachers and principals look like in relation to our students." In a report by *USA Today*, only 7 percent of the nation's teachers are African American. The report also noted that only 1 percent of the nation's teachers are African American men. In promoting TEACH, Duncan said that African Americans and Hispanics comprise 35 percent of the student population in the United States, but only 6 percent to 9 percent of the teachers are African Americans and Hispanics.

In 2008, Stephen Peters, a former school principal who is now a district superintendent in South Carolina, a motivational speaker, and founder of the Gentlemen's Club, cited that less than 1 percent, or fewer than two hundred, of South Carolina's 20,300 elementary school teachers are African American. Nationally, most teachers are Caucasian females. Many times, Caucasian female teachers have a difficult time relating to African American males because they are disconnected from African American males and cannot relate to their upbringing. In many cases, some Caucasian and middle-class African American female teachers are fearful and misunderstand African American male behaviors, including the way they look, talk, walk, act, and dress. It is not surprising that many Caucasian and middle-class African American female teachers appear to have higher expectations for Caucasian and middle-class students than African American male students.

In an effort to increase the number of African American men in the teaching profession, the Call Me MISTER program was started at Clemson University in South Carolina. MISTER stands for Mentors Instructing Students Toward Effective Role Models. Participating college students are mostly selected from educationally and socioeconomically at-risk communities. Through this initiative, participating college students receive loan forgiveness, academic support, and job assistance. The program has enjoyed so much success that Clemson University has partnered with four Historically Black Colleges and Universities in South Carolina to further reach more African American men.

Although there are various programs in place to recruit and retain more men and African American male teachers, classrooms nationwide still struggle to hire them. African American males have few options for relating to someone in the school, in a classroom, or in a leadership position. Often the only African American males in the school are coaches and custodians. If an African American male does not play sports, his chances of having an African American male to serve as a father figure, advisor, or mentor are significantly less. In my studies as a graduate student, much of the evidence I read concluded that African American male students benefit from exposure to teachers who look like them and who can identify with their culture. However, with fewer African American men in the teaching profession, it is essential that schools and school districts aggressively involve as many as they can through volunteerism, during and/or after school.

In relation to African American males, there are not many black educational role models, and often those who are might be too busy with other endeavors to help a youth. Many rappers, entertainers, and professional athletes do not want the role-model label. Unfortunately, many parents, through their actions, are bypassing role model status as well. An African American male who enters his teenage years without a father, a role model, or a caring adult will constantly be trying to find himself. In his findings, Dr. Pedro Noguera supported the idea of most psychiatrists that boys raised without fathers or models of positive manhood are far more likely to express their masculinity and frustrations violently. Furthermore, they become victims to the negative trappings of the street culture and easy targets for street gangs. Through his journey, he may come to believe he can become a man through "being hard" or tough, which may lead to controlling his peers and disrespecting females.

No Child Left Behind (NCLB), signed into law by President George Bush, and the Elementary and Secondary Education Act (ESEA), initiated under President Lyndon Johnson's administration, revitalized by President Barack Obama's Every Student Succeeds Act (ESSA), have made the task of educating African American male students even more challenging. NCLB emphasized that every child—regardless of income, gender, race, ethnicity, or disability—can learn, and that every child deserves to learn. According to NCLB, standardized tests and school choice are major initiatives, and efforts toward reforming American schools must be focused on ensuring that student achievement and learning improve.

Under the NCLB legislation, administrators and teachers were not allowed to exempt underprivileged and disadvantaged groups, such as at-risk African American male students, in meeting NCLB's demanding goals. ESSA, under the Obama administration, has placed a strong commitment for all subgroups to meet the standard in English Language Arts, math, and graduation rates. The revised ESSA has also made college and career readiness through Common Core State Standards a priority. With the United States trailing many first-world nations in educating today's youth, African American males, more than any other subgroup, urgently need strategies and interventions for overcoming obstacles to healthy development and achievement.

Mentoring can be such a strategy and intervention. In chapter 6, I will discuss the **definition of mentoring** and the role it can play in helping African American male students.

Chapter 6
MENTORING

STATISTICS INDICATE THAT so many youth, particularly African American males, have a desperate need for positive role models. The most striking change over recent decades is the structure of the American family, specifically the increasing number of single-parent families as opposed to two-parent families. In 2009, the Let Each One Teach One organization reported that African American youth in America, especially males, have an urgent need for the advancement of strategies and interventions for overcoming obstacles to healthy development and achievement. Mentoring can be one of those strategies and interventions. Mentoring has played an important role in the lives of many boys.

According to authors Terry Neu and Rich Weinfeld in *Helping Boys Succeed in School*, "A mentor is an experienced and trusted advisor who provides a trusting relationship and safe environment and is known for being available to answer life's difficult questions." Mentoring should be a continuous relationship between a youth and an adult. Through continued involvement, the adult provides support, guidance, and assistance as the younger person deals with a challenging time. Mentoring can also be a relationship in which one person who has more experience advises the other of lesser experience. Mentors can have a huge influence, through their guidance and assistance, on their mentees. They can foster a safe, caring, and trusting environment. In relation to African American males, mentors can inspire them to stay in school and attend college or get a good job. Through mentoring, African American males can be exposed to positive practices. Schools can use mentoring to help offset the barriers and challenges that are often noted with African American male students. Specifically, in schools with limited African American educators, mentoring can foster stronger relationships between school personnel and African American males and disprove the negative images often associated with them.

Leading researchers have recognized the importance of mentors establishing a level of comfort and possessing knowledge, wisdom, experience, and some level of disciplinary expertise. Ultimately mentoring is more than acting as a counselor. There are many reasons for becoming a mentor. In *The Mentor's Guide: Facilitating Effective Learning Relationships*, Lois Zachary noted these reasons as (a) the satisfaction of passing on knowledge, (b) increasing one's own productivity, and (c) being in a position to exert positive influence. Zachary stated that mentors need to be comfortable using a wide range of skills. Such skills include (a) building and maintaining relationships, (b) coaching, (c) communicating, (d) encouraging, (e) facilitating, (f) goal setting, (g) guiding, (h) managing conflict, (i) problem-solving, (j) providing and receiving feedback, and (k) reflecting.

I have participated in and initiated several mentoring programs in my life. In working with African American males, I have noted that mentors should be willing to listen, spend time, and commit to making a difference. Unfortunately, I have seen many adults begin mentoring programs but fail to commit to the child. This often leads dedicated mentors to take on more children, decreasing one-to-one time with his or her mentee and minimizing the overall effectiveness of the mentoring program. More importantly, this leads to the child (mentee) being disappointed. Unlike many of my educational colleagues and leading experts on the subject, I do not believe mentors need hours of specialized training or an expensive, complicated, and dressed-up curriculum to serve as role models and advisers to our youth. Costs and complexity can overwhelm prospective mentors and volunteers ready to jump in and help mold and shape the life of an African American male. Simplicity is of the utmost importance with commitment, time, and realness as critical elements.

The purpose of mentoring programs varies from group to group. There is no "one size fits all" concept. Some mentoring programs have an academic, tutoring ,or literacy focus, while others may be geared around individual and character development and career awareness. In 2006, Horace Hall indicated that mentoring is considered to be a relationship where a person with greater experience assists another with less. Such a relationship is typically viewed as one-on-one interaction of non-blood or unrelated individuals of different ages. However, with the increased number of absent adults, mentoring programs have grown in number for the past twenty years. While I challenge all African American men to step up and mentor an African American male, in actuality, mentors can be males of other races or females, and according to Mychal Wynn in his book *Teaching, Parenting, and Mentoring Successful Black Males*, adults such as teachers, guidance counselors, school administrators, or even an older student. The primary focus should be the African American male student being mentored and his development, not who's the mentor.

Mentoring programs for youth are more common with schools but can easily be organized by churches, libraries, or recreation and neighborhood centers. School personnel, church members, fraternal and sorority groups, business and civic leaders, older high school and college students (seeking volunteer hours), and regular citizens who just want to get involved can all be excellent mentors for African American males.

In schools, coaches and teachers usually play important roles in the development of boys. However, Neu and Weinfeld noted that not all coaches and teachers are mentors because they are concerned with developing specific skills, sometimes within the context of a limited time period. It is no secret that most children, including African American males, learn best by watching the behavior and mannerisms of the adults in their lives and by having a chance to apply what they have learned under careful guidance. While skill development is an important part of teaching young men, the relationship component between them and their mentors will determine more long-term success. In his book *The Miracles of Mentoring: The Joy of Investing in Our Future*, Thomas Dortch indicated that "what they see is what they will be" and "we have an obligation to offer them positive role models." Through continued involvement, the adult offers support, guidance, and assistance as the African American male or mentee goes through a difficult period, faces new challenges, or works to correct earlier problems. Mentoring programs are established to meet the needs of African American males and mentees who seem to be at risk regarding societal, academic, or personal issues. Mentoring programs should show kids how to replicate success. They should not be just about material success but total success in their lives.

Therefore, effective mentoring must be a priority in schools, churches, and communities everywhere if we expect African American males to make progress. It must take a supportive arrangement that gives the African American male multiple opportunities to experience success and the eventual ability to interact positively with his peer group, school officials, other adults, and nationalities if we expect him to be globally competitive in the twenty-first century. In chapter 7, I will discuss **various types of mentoring** that might serve as a model for organizing a mentoring program in your school, church, or community.

Chapter 7

TYPES OF MENTORING PROGRAMS

IN GENERAL, MENTORING is best defined as a one-on-one relationship between an adult and youth. According to Terry Neu and Rich Weinfeld in *Helping Boys Succeed in School,* the two types of mentoring programs that are mostly established in schools are **planned mentoring** and **natural mentoring**. Planned mentoring is an occasion where a deliberate attempt is made to match a boy with a mentor. Planned mentorships can be provided by outside organizations or schools to connect boys with mentors for specific projects or for lifelong guidance. In planned mentoring, mentors and participants are selected and matched through formal processes.

Natural mentoring, according to Neu and Weinfeld, is the process of friendship, collegiality, teaching, coaching, and counseling. The natural mentor develops a relationship with the mentee through existing institutions like schools, organized sports programs, neighborhoods, and churches. The natural mentor is placed in the mentee's environment to be a guide for success in life. Natural mentorships can develop within the normal sequence of everyday life. Natural mentorships can come out of nowhere, and on occasion they come from a person who is part of a system.

Regardless of which process is used, it is evident that mentoring plays a critical role. According to Horace Hall in *Mentoring Young Men of Color: Meeting the Needs of African American and Latino Students*, mentoring relationships usually take place over a fixed period of time. They may extend over a school semester while some may go on for months or even years, depending on the function and purpose of the mentor-mentee involvement. In contrast from Neu and Weinfeld, Hall separates mentoring programs into multiple categories, including the classical model and youth mentoring.

In chapter 8, I will discuss **important things to consider** in establishing a mentoring program for African American males.

Chapter 8
Establishing a Mentoring Program

Evidence suggests that planning and structuring are key components in beginning a mentoring program. Horace Hall summarized the importance of space in mentoring young men of color. In the mentoring programs I have facilitated, I used large areas that allowed for plenty of movement and activity. For example, as a mentor in an elementary after-school program with my fraternity, Omega Psi Phi, the cafeteria was reserved for academic assistance while the gymnasium was used for recreation after homework was completed. As a former teacher who sponsored an after-school mentoring program for African American boys, I used my classroom for tutorial help. However, my mentees and I would go outside for free play after our academic focus. Hall wrote that they need "space to move around and assemble, where they can express who they are without being labeled ... where they can strive to understand themselves in the context of the world around them, and where they can inhale and then release."

Generally, schools are more than willing to open up their doors for mentoring, during and after school, especially if there is an academic component involved. As a principal, I was happy to make the building available to fraternities, sororities, nonprofit groups, and college and community volunteers. The key was to make sure days and hours were posted and advertised so that an appropriate, certified school official could be available in the building for liability purposes. Motivational speaker and author Stephen Peters acknowledged that schools must take appropriate steps to ensure that boys can express their thoughts and opinions in an open way. In 2005, I founded a group called the CAGERS©. The group afforded professional and retired men opportunities to visit and mentor young men during and after school. CAGERS© stands for character education, athletic competition, gang awareness, educational services, recruiting support, and service to the community©. In this organization, adult male mentors and I used the SHARE curriculum to guide discussions with our young male participants. SHARE stands for self-efficacy, honesty, attitude, respect, and etiquette. These focus areas served as our topics of discussion and provided our participants with meaningful conversation to help them with their personal and social development. For example, each mentoring session focused on one of the components from the SHARE curriculum, culminating with a guest speaker who wanted to help but did not have the time to devote to regular mentoring. The speaking sessions were interactive with a lot of dialogue between the speaker and the African American male participants.

I always believed in my mentoring experiences that opportunities to talk freely within a meaningful framework were important for African American boys. This provided them with the trust and security they needed to be comfortable. Michael Gurian and Kathy Stevens in their book *The Minds of Boys: Saving Our Sons from Falling Behind in School and Life* hinted that boys also need to have a safe haven at school where they can express vulnerable emotions. They claimed that boys can learn if those around them care about their education.

Hall also stated that safety in constructing such a space must be a priority. He further noted that spaces must be free from psychological and physical violence, judgment, ridicule, and disrespect, especially if African American boys open up and share personal feelings and information. Serving as a mentor to African American boys, I can't express enough the importance of listening and speaking in a relationship with the mentee. Lois Zachary shared in *The Mentor's Guide: Facilitating Effective Learning Relationships* that mentors can monitor the communication that takes place by "(a) actively listening, (b) checking out assumptions about what is going on periodically, (c) sharing thoughts and feelings, (d) maintaining sensitivity about the mentee's personal and learning needs, (e) discussing accountability and following up regularly, (f) reflecting on the learning taking place, and (g) focusing on the mentee's learning goals."

When I met with mentees for the first time, I generally shared some information about me so they could relax. I had them complete a short interest inventory so I could learn what they like. Typically, with African American boys, I hook them by talking about my athletic background and sports teams that I like. I do this to make them feel comfortable so future conversations are easier. Sports is not my focus in the long term, but I found that it could get me in the door for them to open up. I have seen other mentors connect through discussing popular television shows that mentees might watch or music that is hip. As Zachary wrote, "Becoming culturally aware, developing a working knowledge of and appreciation of other cultures, and becoming culturally attuned to other cultures are other essential steps a mentor must learn and possess." Opening a mentoring session with African American boys by discussing western civilization or William Shakespeare would be a disaster because it would not interest them. It is important for the mentor or speaker to engage African American boys or mentees "where they are" and with topics they can relate to so they will feel comfortable.

Relevance is important to African American boys. They can relate to real life. Any mentoring curriculum that is used at a school, church, or recreation or neighborhood center should contain a social and cultural emphasis sensitive to their background. Hall expressed it best when he said, "It must inform them of what is happening in the world around them, draw connections from those events in their life and enlighten them as to the various choices that they can make and the consequences of those decisions." African American boys also like the arts, so a strong mentoring program should provide such opportunities. Most African American boys like to sing, dance, and/or act. During mentoring programs that I have facilitated, I allowed my mentees to rap or role-play messages about making positive choices or avoiding drugs and alcohol use. These examples of self-expression provide African American boys with confidence in being themselves and appreciation for their creativity.

Today, with such a large focus on college and career readiness and Common Core State Standards, a strong mentoring program for African American boys should emphasize reading and writing with career and college awareness. During my mentoring sessions, I engage mentees through quick writes in their reflective journals before we begin discussions. topics might be as simple as these:

1. Imagine a time in your life when you were disrespected. Describe what happened and how you responded. What did you learn from the situation? Explain how different the world would be if we all respected each other.
2. In your opinion, do you think Michael Vick's actions with dogfighting should have led to a prison term and suspension from the NFL? Why or why not? If you were the NFL commissioner, would you let Vick or other players who break the law play again?
3. Some rules in school make students upset and seem unnecessary at times. If you were in charge, which rule would you keep? Which would you not keep? What new rule would you add and how might it benefit students?

African American boys do not have enough writing opportunities, especially beyond the classroom. In this age of cell phone texting and social media messaging, communication is often short or in broken English. In reference to books, too many teachers are caught up in the genre. African American boys should be encouraged to read any age-appropriate book or magazine that interests them. My classroom library featured a variety of magazines and books for African American boys to choose from when they needed to read after finishing their assignments early. I brought and purchased *Ebony, Boy's Life, Sports Illustrated, Sports Illustrated for Kids, Vibe, The Source, Slam Dunk,* and *Jet* magazines for leisure reading. While some of the readings were not something I personally liked, I knew from their interest surveys that they liked them. The most important thing is that they were reading and had consistent opportunities to practice reading, especially in an age when we as a society are competing against Netflix, video games, Facebook, Twitter, Instagram, and other forms of entertainment.

Reading and writing performance has been used as a major predictor of future imprisonment in America. In his 2007 publication, *Teaching, Parenting, and Mentoring Successful Black Males,* Mychal Wynn recommended the following to improve writing and literacy through mentoring programs:

1. Integrate reading, writing, and book reports into your strategies of character, moral, intellectual, and spiritual development.
2. Monitor reading proficiency and standardized reading, writing, and language scores.
3. Create a literacy-rich environment by keeping books wherever there are young men.
4. Assign weekly book reports.
5. Build reading time into a mentoring program.

In chapter 9, I will discuss **ways to create the ideal mentoring culture** to promote success for African American males.

Chapter 9

CREATING A POSITIVE MENTORING CULTURE

SOME MENTORING PROGRAMS are successful and others are unsuccessful. In creating a positive mentoring program for African American boys, it should be structured to be sustained over a given period of time and to provide opportunities for mentors to listen to their mentees' thoughts and feelings and do things together. Mentoring programs that contain these areas of emphasis in their framework tend to do well while those without these components only last for a limited period of time. Creating a positive mentoring culture also is dependent on the motivation of the mentors. Lois Zachary shared in *The Mentor's Guide: Facilitating Effective Learning Relationships* that motivation has an impact on sustainability and commitment, and she pointed out that the difference between successful and unsuccessful mentoring programs lies in sustainability. Zachary also noted that mentoring programs enjoy sustainability when mentoring is embedded in an organizational culture that values continuous learning.

As a district administrator, I began Lunch Buddies programs at two schools with a high number of at-risk students. I asked guidance counselors from both schools to identify students who could benefit from mentoring. The Lunch Buddies program was a school-based mentoring program that took place during the school day. Mentors included local business, church, and school leaders who gave up a normal lunch every two weeks to eat lunch with an at-risk student. Before mentors began participating in the Lunch Buddies program, an orientation was provided to explain expectations, including dates of the program and commitment requirements. A similar orientation was provided for students and their parents. To support the sustainability aspect of the program, mentors were paired with students over a two-year period. For example, at the targeted elementary school, mentors started in the Lunch Buddies program when mentees were in fourth grade. This mentoring relationship continued in fifth grade to build on the relationships between the mentor and mentee. Such consistent and ongoing contact within the school is very important. It is critical that school leaders organize regular contact between mentors and mentees.

In creating a mentoring program that focuses on African American males, an important emphasis should be placed on the mentors and mentees doing things together. Earlier in chapter one, I discussed a group of young men called Technique that I worked with when I was a young teacher. While mentoring sessions focused on character development at the school, we spent a great deal of time doing things together. For example, we went to a nursing home and played bingo with elderly residents. In addition, we played basketball regularly at an old gymnasium downtown. And, as I mentioned in chapter one, we watched the Super Bowl together with parental permission.

Later in my career as a junior high school teacher, I organized an after-school mentoring group called the Marvelous Monday Mentoring Club. The purpose of the group was to increase the academic achievement of eighth grade African American boys through mentoring, with an emphasis on efficacy. While the curriculum focused on academic skills through efficacy programs and mentoring relationships, an integral part of the program was bonding activities off campus. We went to a pizza restaurant together, played pool, and watched a movie at a local theater. As an assistant principal, I mentored a group of young men as well. We also went to eat at a local restaurant where etiquette was a major focus area. Along with other mentors from the mentoring program, we attended a college basketball game with the mentees.

During both of my principalships, I facilitated a mentoring program called the Young Gents. The purpose of this mentoring program was to improve behavior and academic achievement through character development. The participating mentors and I wanted the African American male students whom we worked with to feel good about themselves and make better choices. The young men were required to wear a shirt and tie on designated days each week. Shirts, ties, and belts were donated by mentors and local churches. As a high school principal, I accompanied my Young Gents to a domestic violence workshop in relation to teenage dating with local law enforcement officers off campus. We also visited a Historical Black College and University (HBCU), ate at Golden Corral restaurant, and attended a NBA game between the Miami Heat and the Charlotte Bobcats (now Hornets).

As a measure to improve behavior and grades, we told the mentees upfront where we would be going. However, they could only have a limited number of referrals and no grade less than C if they planned to attend. Many of the toughest African American boys, whom no other teacher wanted, earned the opportunity to go on this trip. I was a proud principal as I witnessed the excitement on the faces of so many African American boys who had never been to a nice restaurant or a professional sports contest, or on a college visit. Probably the greatest satisfaction came when several of the young men, who did not have college aspirations before the trip, started to take school more seriously, applied for the HBCU that we visited, and were accepted to attend the institution. Through the Young Gents mentoring program, the mentors and I built trust with the mentees, and we changed mind-sets and lives. Only through doing things with the mentees did they have these kinds of opportunities that they will never forget. Through the Young Gents, the mentors and I developed strategies that considered the African American boys' culture, learning styles, and issues that challenged them and the action steps to make them successful.

Creating a positive mentoring culture for African American males also hinges on building a strong relationship with them and their families. Barry MacDonald pointed out in his 2005 book, *Boy Smarts: Mentoring Boys for Success at School*, that friendships are impacted by mentoring, especially from boys to men. Mentoring then is important in identity development, self-esteem, and self-perception.

A big reason for these strong relationships was the connections we made with the families. We communicated with parents and families regularly by text, e-mail, social media, phone calls, and face-to-face meetings. Athletic competitions (basketball in this case) was a major part of the mentoring program. When mentees participated in tournaments across the Southeast, their parents and families were extended invitations. As we ate at restaurants during our travels, parents and families also dined with us. Annually, we attended an NBA game with the mentees and their parents and families. During a college visit to a major university in Florida, parents and families were invited to take the tour with the mentees, mentors, and myself. Admissions counselors provided information to mentees and parents.

As the mentoring relationships with the young men of CAGERS© have developed over the years, some mentees frequently stay at my home with my own son (who is also part of the mentoring program), family, and me. During the school year, I attend their middle and high school games. They glowed as I walked into the gym or football stadium to watch them compete. Equally, I am excited to be there to support them because I know how much it means to them. During the week, we checked in with each other with a simple text. Text exchanges end with "love you" and "much love." They also communicated this way with each other through messaging by cell phone, Facebook, Instagram, Twitter, Snapchat, or other forms of social media. These forms of expression were strong examples that African American boys, despite the hardness they had to carry on the outside, are sensitive individuals who want to feel loved and valued.

The parents and families know that their young men are mentored and directed by men who empathize with them. They know that we want to serve. Most of the CAGERS©' mentors are African American men who share similar backgrounds and experiences as the African American males who participate in the program. Programs like CAGERS© that I have been involved with seek to support school activities by providing a positive presence of African American men. Although CAGERS© has had men of other nationalities involved, most of the mentors have been African American men. In CAGERS©, African American men serve as mentors, coaches, and father figures with goals of providing African American boys with support and guidance.

Mentoring programs like CAGER.©, Young Gents, Marvelous Monday Mentoring Program, Technique, and LifeQuest have assisted at-risk African American boys in dealing with the hostile and unfortunate conditions that have established them as a group in crisis. From my own experiences as a mentor, African American boys benefit from mentoring programs, be it at school, church, or recreation or neighborhood centers. They tend to be close to their mentors on an even greater basis, beyond the actual mentoring setting, when meaningful and relevant activities are planned. With so many absent fathers in the African American family and community, it is vital that other African American men get involved. It does not matter if they already have children that they raise or if they have already "graduated" their children. With the current crisis of African American boys, African American men can help overcome the odds as mentors and complement single-mother households as father figures, adopted daddies, or surrogate dads or uncles.

In chapter 10, I will discuss some **well-known mentoring programs** in the United States in which African American men and other men who want to volunteer can get involved. Through involvement in such mentoring programs, they can connect with African American boys and help them overcome the challenges they face.

Chapter 10

MENTORING PROGRAMS

NATIONALLY, SEVERAL MENTORING programs are making an effort to relate to at-risk youth, such as African American males. These mentoring programs concentrate on such areas as social and life skills, character development, academic support, and career and college readiness. The mentoring programs for African American male students vary widely. Some are school based while others occur after school. Some occur away from the school but work with school officials to make sure the targeted population is transported to the appropriate setting. Some programs are specific for African American males only, but many are not.

With female-dominated classrooms and households, many African American boys need additional support beyond the classroom. More African American male teachers would be ideal to help them with identity development. However, as mentioned in earlier chapters, African American men are a rarity in most school systems. Despite the shortage in the classroom, mentoring and mentoring programs are outstanding opportunities for African American men to get involved as mentors, speakers, chaperones, and volunteers.

There are several examples of mentoring programs that can serve as models for schools, churches, and recreation or neighborhood centers, and interested individuals who desire to become involved. Some have been around for decades; others are relatively new. However, each has been successful in addressing the needs of African American males and at-risk youth.

BIG BROTHERS BIG SISTERS OF AMERICA

Perhaps one of the most recognizable programs nationally is Big Brothers Big Sisters. Terry Neu and Rich Weinfeld noted in *Helping Boys Succeed in School* that this organization has served more than two hundred thousand children, ages eight to eighteen, in five thousand communities across all fifty states. Founded in 1904, the program is well developed and has a deep understanding of the specifics needed for men to be good mentors. Big Brothers Big Sisters matches at-risk youth with older volunteer mentors. The major emphasis is on continuity and consistency in mentoring relationships. In a 2007 report, "Making a Difference in Schools: The Big Brothers Big Sisters School-Based Mentoring Impact Study," Carla Herrera, Jean Baldwin Grossman, Tina Kauh, Amy Feldman, Jennifer McMaken, and Linda Jucovy evaluated Big Brothers Big Sisters of America and found that there were significant improvements in participants' academic performance, perceived scholastic efficacy, school misconduct, and attendance relative to non-mentored youth. Following up the study in a 2011 profile, Carla Herrera, Jean Baldwin Grossman, Tina Kauh, and Jennifer McMaken indicated that participants were 46 percent less likely to begin using illegal drugs, 27 percent less likely to begin using alcohol, 52 percent less likely to skip school, and 35 percent less likely to be involved in a physical confrontation at school. The authors noted that participating minority students, such as African Americans, were less likely to initiate drug use when compared to their non-mentored peers. Overall, the participants were more confident in their schoolwork performance, were able to demonstrate modest gains in their grade point averages, and were able to get along better with their families.

MENTORING THE 100 WAY

A planned mentoring program that has had a positive impact on African American males is Mentoring the 100 Way, a program of the 100 Black Men of America, Inc. Thomas Dortch, the 100 Black Men's president, shared in *The Miracles of Mentoring: The Joy of Investing in the Future* that this program shows kids how to replicate success—not just material success but total success in their lives. The 100 Black Men of America started in New York in the early 1960s. This group of African American lawyers, physicians, educators, civic leaders, entrepreneurs, and government leaders has several programs across the country, established to mentor young African American males.

The 100 Black Men of America, Inc., website noted that Mentoring the 100 Way addresses the following: (a) the social, (b) emotional, and (c) cultural needs of children ages eight to eighteen. Members are trained and certified to become mentors, advocates, and role models for the youth within their communities. Through chapter-operated one-to-one and group mentoring efforts, members forge relationships that positively impact youth. The program focuses on building a combination of skills, including character building, goal setting, peer-to-peer mentoring, conflict resolution, and leadership development. Dortch noted that 100 Black Men of America, Inc., has more than one hundred thousand youth participants annually in its mentoring and youth development programs. The mentoring programs have been recognized nationally as models of success because they use a rigorous training and evaluation system.

Mychal Wynn reported in *Empowering African-American Males: A Guide to Increasing Black Male Achievement* that the 100 Black Men of America identify the same youth over an extended period of time to provide continuity in their programs. Structured tutoring programs are common as well as opportunities for youth to obtain scholarships and financial assistance. Wynn found that the 100 Black Men of America organization provides an important association among middle and high school African American youth and positive African American men.

Let Each One Teach One

This mentoring organization is specifically for at-risk African American male adolescents. According to the Let Each One Teach One website, the goals of this program center on increasing the academic success of students. The program measures its effectiveness by monitoring improved grades, enhanced self-efficacy, improved behavioral conduct, improved self-perception, fewer office referrals and suspensions, and improved attendance.

Let Each One Teach One uses the relationship between an elementary or middle school student and an older, more experienced student role model to provide life-skills and self-image enrichment, support, and a sense of belonging. Mentors help participants set personal and academic goals. The participants' study skills are assessed, and the mentors provide methods for helping them learn and remember what was discussed in class, plan and write papers, learn methods for math assignments, prepare for a test, complete homework, and improve study at home. According to Let Each One Teach One, mentors model how they accomplished these things and explore with students a plan for doing the same. Visualization procedures are used to help students envision themselves as more successful.

Jack and Jill of America, Inc.

The largest and oldest African American family organization in the United States is Jack and Jill of America, Inc. Jack and Jill of America exposes African American students and their families to cultural, social, civic, and recreational activities. Founded by Louise Dench and Marion Thomas, with the involvement of several mothers, Jack and

Jill of America allows nonmember teenagers to participate in many social experiences. Such interaction through conferences, camps, and balls is a major emphasis. The organization has seven regions and an annual teenage convention. It appeals to upper- and middle-class families while focusing some programs on disadvantaged youth.

THE HARLEM EDUCATIONAL ACTIVITIES FUND

The Harlem Educational Activities Fund (HEAF) was founded by Daniel and Joanna Rose. According to the HEAF website, the founders believe that any kid of reasonable intelligence, regardless of their family background, can become an academic success given enough guidance, effort, and time. No matter how poor a student may be, poverty is not seen as an insurmountable obstacle. HEAF is located in Harlem, New York. The walls of HEAF are covered with inspirational paraphernalia, college acceptance letters, pictures, and axioms.

Daniel Rose, a middle-aged man, advocated for HEAF to act as a tutor, surrogate parent, and godfather coaching students for competitive high school and college entry exams, training them in leadership, and counseling them on personal problems. Participants are provided with blazers for college interviews and computers when they go to college if they keep their grades up.

THE EFFICACY INSTITUTE

An exemplary program is the Efficacy Institute's Efficacy Curriculum. Dr. Jeff Howard, the organization's president, founded the Efficacy Institute. Howard developed the efficacy program to understand the psychology of success. It is a training and consulting firm dedicated to the belief that intelligence is a developmental process, not something that is fixed at birth or by socioeconomic or cultural factors. I discovered in gathering information from the North Central Regional Educational Laboratory (NCREL) that a team wrote the Efficacy Institute's curriculum. The members of the team were Howard, Barney Brawer, Jesse Soloman, Verna Ford, Eugene Wade, and Joyce Swagert. Self-efficacy, which is an individual's ability to accomplish his or her goals, is a major part of Howard's Efficacy Institute and self-efficacy curriculum. Ultimately, an individual's experiences drive his or her effort to take on challenging tasks.

The NCREL stated that the Efficacy Institute's platform is it is not enough to believe all children can learn. The education reform organization also believes that all children can learn whatever they need to in order to become highly developed adults. In his 2002 article, "The Third Movement: Developing African American Children for the 21st Century," Howard commented that adults need to take responsibility for showing young people why they should become committed to their own development, for teaching them how to do it, and then for managing their process. Efficacy provides a model to teach children how to develop themselves and the framework to teach educators and other adults how to create and maintain environments that support the development of children.

As I indicated in chapter 8, in the CAGERS© organization, adult male mentors and I used the SHARE curriculum to guide discussions with our young male participants. SHARE stands for self-efficacy, honesty, attitude, respect, and etiquette. Self-efficacy is our first area of focus because, as Howard elaborated, people who feel good about themselves attribute their success to their ability and effort and their failure solely to effort. We want the African American males we mentor to understand that their success is dependent on the amount of time they put into the area in which they need to improve. We do not want failure to constitute them giving up, which is often what they do in relation to academics. As they would do in learning plays in sports or remembering lyrics with rap music, we want them to recognize that their effort and time on task leads to better outcomes. Howard further clarified that the Efficacy Institute has had some success with increasing the confidence and efficacy of African American males, which has fostered improved academic performance.

In summary, the Efficacy Institute seeks to assist all youth who are struggling academically, regardless of their race or culture, by training educators and parents. Educators and parents receive training on approaches to help build confidence, increase effort, and educate all by high standards.

GENTLEMEN'S CLUB

The Gentlemen's Club was formed by Stephen Peters, a former classroom teacher and middle school principal who is now an author and motivational speaker, originally from South Carolina. As a principal and district administrator, I have had the wonderful experience of listening to Peters's presentations at several workshops in and out of the school districts in which I have worked. He has become nationally known for working with teachers and administrators who teach at-risk students. He developed the Gentlemen's Club for building relationships with at-risk African American males prior to them becoming discipline problems. Peters has published several well-known books, such as *Do You Know Enough About Me to Teach Me?* (2006) and *Teaching to Capture and Inspire All Learners: Bringing Your Best Stuff Every Day!* (2007). The Gentlemen's Club was designed to focus on three areas: attendance, behavior, and academic achievement. Peters noted that the curriculum was relevant, inspiring, and practical. He credited the organization's success on the involvement of students and teachers in the design and structure of the program. The curriculum has a strong emphasis on writing and language and provides participants with opportunities to share their experiences and feelings. Peters believes this builds trust, which leads to opening doors of success in primary academic courses, and in turn gives students a reason to come to school.

The Peters's Group website notes that the Gentlemen's Club's success has increased attendance and academic achievement and decreased negative behavior. Peters indicated that sustainability can also be contributed to the active participation of well-trained and committed on-site facilitators. Gentlemen's Clubs have now been established with schools and school districts across the country, in such states as Texas, Ohio, and South Carolina. Each club costs approximately $12,500 per year and is renewable annually at $10,000. Costs include (a) visits by Peters, (b) facilitator training, (c) Gentlemen's Club ties, (d) Gentlemen's Club facilitators' curriculum guides, (e) etiquette lunch or dinner, (f) all travel expenses included in the first year, and (g) Gentlemen's Club certified chapter certificate. If school districts have multiple certified chapters, the cost is two to one for up to ten chapters.

The aforementioned programs are just a select few in supporting the needs of African American males and at-risk youth. New programs are opening monthly to meet the needs of African American males. It is no secret that the African American male is at risk, targeted, and most of all an endangered species. We must put our males at the forefront of our conversations and our concern. The following chapter will summarize research on **single gender** and how it can make a difference.

Chapter 11
ROLE MODELS NEEDED

AFRICAN AMERICAN MALE students continue to be a challenge in our classrooms. While schools have created programs for various reasons, mentoring continues to be the number one goal, particularly for middle school youth. According to research, despite initiatives, schools must continue to find ways to motivate and develop the full academic potential of African American male students. They are pressured by peers and relate less to teachers who do not look like them, female and white. The shortage of black male teachers is a concern in school districts because there are fewer role models for this population of students. As kindergarten through twelfth grade classrooms become more diverse across school districts, exposing students to various role models may be important, according to Gursky (2002). There is a benefit to black males relating to black male teachers.

In relation to gender and race, Noguera (2008) questioned if black men are not around to teach young boys the essence of manhood, fatherhood, and family life, who will? More black men must, out of a sense of urgency, join the ranks of men who are destined to move beyond marches and rhetoric to mentor young men (Noguera, 2008). The educational system and individual classroom are not as well designed for male brain development as for female. It is not uncommon for teachers to share with administrators their preferences for the type of student or gender they prefer. The system is comprised of mainly female teachers who have not received training in male brain development and performance (Wynn, 2005). Given the severity of problems associated with African American males in schools, advocates for race- and gender-exclusive schooling defend such strategies that reorganize the gendered nature of schools and classrooms as the best approach (Martino and Meyenn, 2001). Some black educators have alluded to a national conspiracy to destroy black boys (Kunjufu, 1985).

Some teachers continue to hold lower expectations of black and Hispanic youth and reveal these expectations by giving less praise, encouragement, attention, and interest to these youths (Denbo, 1986).

It is evident that not all children will attend college after high school, but some will attend a technical or community college or trade school, go into the military, or take a job that seeks a high school diploma as the highest academic level earned. What we cannot do as educators, parents, mentors, and even caring adults in our black male youths' lives is push to the point of no return. We have to embrace that females and males learn differently, seek achievement differently, and most of all develop differently. A "one size fits all" approach does not and will not work with our black males. Hall (2006) noted that an all-male mentee and mentor setting does not mean that female mentors are incapable of contributing to male forums. He elaborated, "Quite the contrary, women have much to say that inform males of the conscious and unconscious aspects of masculinity and how it impacts gender relationships" (Hall, 2006, p. 29). It is time for African American men to stand up as fathers and role models to our black youth. They must be the providers and the keepers of our young male students. Noguera (2008) stated it best: mentors should return to their neighborhoods and teach black males how to survive. We so need that today and right now.

In the following chapter, the **summary** will conclude with how we know our world today and what our next steps are.

Summary

I ATTEMPTED TO complete this book with the hope that there would be readers like you who have the passion as William and I have. I am thrilled that this is where his book has come from us to you. Nonetheless, you are reading about a passion that we both share: youth, males, and the African American race. Nothing compares to that, nothing.

My experiences with African American males started early in my teaching career. As a former teacher in an inner-city urban setting, I had to change my way of thinking and learn to teach my boys differently than my girls. My African American boys needed me to nurture them, guide them, and yes, eventually teach them. But before I could do any of that, I had to connect with the whole child, so if that meant having to mentor them with the ideology of sitting at a basketball game on the outside court on Saturday or having Thanksgiving dinner at seven or eight homes on that one important family day, then that is what it was and I did it! My boys needed me, and whatever they needed, I provided. I showed my African American students that there was a way out, and that was through education and finding the one person who supported and guided with words of wisdom.

I have come to learn and love that there are many people in this world who support African American males and want to be their mentor and support system. It takes a strong support team to make this happen, and thus, this book *Mentoring Can Make a Difference* was born. I read a book by Lisa Delpit called *The Skin That We Speak: Thoughts on Language and Culture in the Classroom*. In this book, I read about dialect language, poverty, social skills, and even about the color of our skin and what it means today in society. The great Asa Hilliard III was an inspiration in Delpit's book, and I want to bring up a certain point he made. One of Asa's primary lessons was that, "we must leave no stone unturned, no battle unfought, to allow the brilliance of our children—of children of color—to bring light to the world" (Delpit, 2002, p. iv). This statement was on the very first page of the book. It reminded me that we should reflect and make sure we are putting our students first and giving them the opportunities they deserve and need to be successful in our ever-changing global society. If we are going to be honest and really delve into the problems of our African American youth and what they need, we better discuss the future, the present, and the past because our world is cyclical as we know. We are in 2016, but our world around us represents 1970 or earlier. Black youth are being killed, men are being killed in front of their families, and heroin has resurfaced as the drug of choice, yet we are to trust the local police officer to protect us when usually "blue lives" are the ones who are killing "black lives." When did we color code our lives? What happened to "all lives matter"? When we move our mind-sets from stereotyping every African American we see and get to know the person, then we may be in the same circle of troubles.

Throughout this book you read about what it takes to be a mentor, but more importantly what mentoring is and how it applies to you as an adult working with an African American youth. Remember, young adults are hurt by our words. They are in pain because they hear us talk to one another in a manner that is not conducive to mankind. We have to be proactive to do the right thing, and we have to be respectful to each other. African American youth do not trust us because of our behavior. You cannot remove the skin they are in, but you can adjust your attitude to not prejudge or degrade before getting to know them. Learn what you can, to know all that you can.

References

Blackman, L., O. Clayton, N. Glenn, L. Malone-Colon, and A. Roberts. 2005. "The Consequences of Marriage for African Americans: A Comprehensive Literature Review." New York: Institute for American Values.

Cose, Ellis. 2002. *The Envy of the World: On Being Black in America*. New York: Washington Square Press.

Dappen, L., and J. C. Iserhagen. 2006. "Urban and Nonurban Schools: Examination of a Statewide Student Mentoring Program." *Urban Education*, 41, 151–168.

Delpit, L. and J. Dowdy. 2002. *The Skin That We Speak: Thoughts on Language and Culture in the Classroom*. New York: The New Press.

Denbo, S. 1986. *Improving Minority Student Achievement: Focus on the Classroom*. Washington, DC: Mid-Atlantic Equity Consortium.

Dortch, T. 2000. *The Miracles of Mentoring: The Joy of Investing in Our Future*. New York: Doubleday.

Garrison-Wade, D., and C. Lewis. 2006. "Tips for Principals and Teachers: Helping Black Students Achieve," *White Teachers/Diverse Classrooms*. J. Landsman and C. Lewis, eds. Sterling, VA: Stylus Publishing, LLC, 52-60.

Gurian, M., and K. Stevens. 2005. *The Minds of Boys: Saving Our Sons from Falling Behind in School and Life*. San Francisco: Jossey-Bass.

Gursky, D. (2002). *Recruiting minority teachers: Programs aim to balance quality and diversity in preparing teachers*. Retrieved from: http://www/aft/org/pubsreports/americanteachers/feb02.html

Hall, H. 2006. *Mentoring Young Men of Color: Meeting the Needs of African American and Latino Students.* Lanham, MD: Rowman and Littlefield Publishing Group, Inc.

Herrera, C., J. B. Grossman, T. J. Kauh, A. F. Feldman, and J. McMaken, J. 2011. "Mentoring in Schools: An Impact Study of Big Brothers Big Sisters School-Based Mentoring." *Raising Healthy Children*, 82(1), 346–361. DOI:10.1111/j.1467-8624.2010.01559.x.

Howard, J. 2002. "The Third Movement: Developing Black Children for the 21st Century." Waltham, MA: The Efficacy Institute, Inc.

Jack and Jill Incorporated. 2011. About Us: Our history. Retrieved from http://www.jack-and-jill.org.

Kleinfeld, J. 2009. "The State of American Boyhood." University of Alaska: Springer Science and Business Media.

Kunjufu, J. 1985. *Countering the Conspiracy to Destroy Black Boys*. Chicago: African-American Images.

Kuykendall, C. 2004. *From Rage to Hope: Strategies for Reclaiming Black and Hispanic Students*. Bloomington, IN: National Education Services.

Let Each One Teach One. 2009. Program Overview. Retrieved from http://www.promisingpractices.net.

Lewis, S., C. Simon, R. Uzzell, A. Howitz, and M. Casserly. 2010. "A Call for Change: The Social and Educational Factors Contributing to the Outcomes of Black Males in Urban Schools." Washington DC: The Council of the Great City Schools.

Martino, W. and B. Weyenn. 2001. *What About the Boys? Issues of Masculinity in Schools*. Philadelphia: Open University Press.

MacDonald, B. 2005. *Boy Smarts: Mentoring Boys for Success at School*. British Columbia, CA: Mentoring Boys Press.

National Center for Education Statistics 2010. Status of Drop Out Rates. Retrieved June 20, 2015, from http://nces.ed.gov/fastfacts/display.asp?id=16.

Neu, T., and R. Weinfeld. 2007. *Helping Boys Succeed in School*. Waco, TX: Prufock Press, Inc.

Noguera, P. 2003. "The Trouble with Black Boys: The Role and Influence of Environmental and Cultural Factors on the Academic Performance of African American Males." *Urban Education*, 38, 431–459.

Noguera, P. 2008. *The Trouble with Black Boys: And Other Reflections on Race, Equity, and the Future of Public Education*. San Francisco: Jossey-Bass.

Norton, R. 2006. "Call Me Mister: A Program that Recruits, Trains, Certifies, and Secures Employment for African American Men as Teachers." Retrieved June 21, 2015, from http://www.black-collegian.com/career/career-reports/mister-grad05.html

"100 Men of America". 2008. Mentoring the 100 Way Retrieved from http://100blackmen.org/mentoring

Peters, S. 2007. *Teaching to Capture and Inspire All Learners: Bringing Your Best Stuff Every Day.* Thousand Oaks, CA: Corwin Press.

Raley, K., and Bumpass, L. 2003. "The topography of the divorce plateau: Levels and trends in union stability in the United States after 1980." Retrieved February 23, 2014 from http://liberalarts.utexas.edu/etag/_files/pdfs/articles/2003/Raley%20and%20Bumpass%202003.ppf.

The Sentencing Project 2009. Incarcerated parents and their children. Retrieved from http://www.sentencingproject.org/doc/publications/publications/inc_incacerated-parents.pdf.

Thermstrom, A., and S. Thermstrom. 2004. *No Excuses: Closing the Racial Gap in Learning.* New York: Simon & Schuster Paperback.

Toldson, I. 2012. "Debunking Education Myths about Blacks." Retrieved June 20, 2015, from http://www.theroot.com/articles/culture/2012/07/black_education_statistics_separating_fact_from_fiction/.

United States Department of Education. 2009. No Child Left Behind. Retrieved October 19, 2015, from http://www.ed.gov/offices/ESE/eses/exec-summ.html.

Wynn, M. 2007. *Teaching, Parenting, and Mentoring Successful Black Males.* Marietta, GA: Rising Sun Publishing, Inc.

Zachary, L. 2000. *The Mentor's Guide: Facilitating Effective Learning Relationships.* San Francisco: Jossey-Bass.

www.ingramcontent.com/pod-product-compliance
Lightning Source LLC
Chambersburg PA
CBHW082151290526
45794CB00008B/3246